RUINED MUSIC

Ruined Music

poems

Valentina Gnup

GRAYSON BOOKS
West Hartford, Connecticut
graysonbooks.com

Ruined Music
Copyright © 2024 by Valentina Gnup
Published by Grayson Books
West Harford, Connecticut
ISBN: 979-8-9888186-4-9
Library of Congress Control Number: 2024931769

Interior & cover design: Cindy Stewart
Cover image: Nude Lying on Bed by Anders Zorn
Author photo by M.P. Moxon

For my daughters, Sophie and China,
you mean what love means to me forever

Acknowledgments

Grateful acknowledgment is made to the editors of the following journals in which these poems or earlier versions of them originally appeared:

Arizona Daily Star: "Czech Angels"

The Best American Poetry, Blog: "American Meditation"

Chelsea: "At Edward Hopper's Self-Portrait," "The Animal Dark" as "Autumn Nocturne," "Dark Red Leaves"

Cutthroat Journal of the Arts: "France Étude"

Crosswinds Poetry Journal: "Two for Joy"

December: "Pink Peonies"

Five South: "Pieces of Days"

HOLE IN THE HEAD re:VIEW: "Song for Ukraine"

International Literary Quarterly: "How to Survive Online Dating," "The Language of Waitresses, 1979," "When We Were Horses," "More Than Sparrows"

The Lascaux Review: "When You Are Invisible, You Can Say Anything"

The Lyre: "Lament of a Bare Branch," "France Étude," "Her Face, Crimson Petals," "The Animal Dark" as "Autumn Aubade," "The Cries of One Crow"

MARY: A Journal of New Writing, Saint Mary's College: "Lament of a Bare Branch," "Shadows in Gold"

Mudfish: "Like Any Woman" as "Hotel Aubade"

The New Guard Review: "On the Corner of Powell and César Chávez"

Nuclear Age Peace Foundation website (wagingpeace.org): "The Cries of One Crow"

Rattle: "A Thousand Possible Clouds," "We Speak of August," "It's a Sad Story," "Another Morning at the Welfare Office" as "Morning at the Welfare Office"

Solo Cafe 2: "Dark Red Leaves"

Two Hawks Quarterly: "The Work of Flying"

The WB Yeats Society of NY website (yeatssociety.nyc)*:* "Doll, It All Goes by So Fast"

These poems appeared in the following anthologies:

Corners of the Mouth: A Celebration of Thirty Years of the Annual SLO Poetry Festival: "The Cries of One Crow"

Kakalak, An Anthology of North and South Carolina Writers: "Her Face, Crimson Petals"

Nothing But Red: "Her Face, Crimson Petals"

***

Thank you to Ginny Connors, publisher of Grayson Books, for her hard work and patience with all my requests, and to Brad Davis for selecting this manuscript and writing about it so generously.

If my mother were still here, she would send this book to her long list of friends and fellow opera fans. I'm grateful to Elle for all the years she lovingly supported my art.

I'm also wildly grateful to Brendan Constantine for his enthusiastic support in all ways. Several of these poems were begun in his *A Tendency to Exist* and other writing workshops. I'm also deeply grateful to Julie Maloney for her encouragement and for showing up in NYC. Several of these poems were begun in her *Women Reading Aloud* workshop.

Abigail Brandt has been a lifetime sister poet. She invited me to my first writing workshop over thirty years ago, and through her, I met other wonderfully talented and supportive poets/friends including David Oliveira, Kathee Miller, Perie Longo, Chryss Yost, Marty Williams, and the late Jackson Wheeler. Several of these poems were started in our twice-monthly distance writing group.

Many poets and writers influenced me at Antioch University Los Angeles, and I am especially grateful to Susan Rich, K.D. Harryman, Tim Seibles, David Trinidad, Amy Gerstler, Frank X. Gaspar, and Elizabeth Austen. Thank you to other amazing poets in various workshops over the years, some who are here and some who are no longer with us—Joy Harjo, Brenda Hillman, Quincy Troupe, Eavan Boland, William Stafford, and Carolyn Kizer.

Many people have carried me through the best and worst of times—but I have to send love to Susan and Marty Brennan-Sawyer, Mary Pat and John Moxon, Jill Shinkle, Andrea Oppedisano, Heidi Robins, Kathy Ortega, Mary Thieme, Jillian Haeseler, Anne and Greg Kirsch, Joe Leadem, Lee Ann Engle, Sheila Lynch, Susan Dell'Osso, and a huge thank you to Elise Marks for her editing help.

Finally, I have learned so much and been inspired by countless students over the years—way too many to name, but I am so grateful for the time we shared.

Contents

MIDNIGHT

MORNING

Give me a world, you have taken the world I was.
—Anne Carson, *O Small Sad Ecstasy of Love*

France Étude

All across Normandy I study the sex of the statues,
women with their two mouths—their insatiable hunger,

their endless mosaic of words. Men with their two heads—
to think of themselves twice? A fool, I question God

even as he holds me up, even as he tosses me back,
my life brief as a mackerel's. Outside the cathedral

a mourning dove performs its hollow music of wind,
barleycorn, and sorrow. The rain comes again, tentative

as a girl's voice—*you are here now, you are here.* There
are doors you close only once, the way the world disappears

one artist at a time—a lace-maker of Alençon stitching
by window light, delicate snowflakes gathering in her lap.

The Animal Dark

A sparrow mistakes my window for sky, shattering glass,
feathers, and blood—death builds its house wherever it wants.

Mystics believe sorrow takes seven years to reach the soul,
our histories enter us while we crack an egg into a skillet

or stand on our porch watching leaves disappear inside
the rusty bed of a truck. Our work is to record the flawed world

—I wanted to save this night, our mouths moving
like moth wings, dusting one another's shoulders, bellies,

and thighs, but daylight stole the foreign and familiar lines
we mapped on each other's skin late in the animal dark.

Ruined Music

I open my encyclopedia of ex-husbands
and lost ghosts, the choir of voices I carry in my head,
to teach you the wisdom of all my mistakes.

I know how to squat and push,
how to reach down and discover
the hard slick head of my infant
descending into the light of one life.

I know the tomatoes and rumpled sheets,
the warm legs and sorrow of a marriage.

I've been a daughter to a mother
who lost a mother too early,

I've been a deer in the tall wheat
that blows like a girl's hair
in golden unison along the Czech highway—
the secrets of the wheat are my secrets.

Lean in closer, turn your best ear to this adagio,
to this harmonica of August—

I'm dangerous. I have longed for people
who would make me a criminal,
I have wasted countless hours, priceless years.

You ask what to call the music
of this impossible yearning—
hold the notes on your tongue,
taste the magnificent, awful song I was.

In the Middle of a Morning

after Marc Chagall's *I and the Village*

We leave each other holding only a bouquet of words.
Isn't every nest temporary?

In the middle of our lives we lose parents,
surrender the tall trees of our children,
walk away from houses, villages, jobs—

like the dog becoming faithful to the goat,
we choose the wrong people.
Who is born holy?

A man with arms stained the deep jade of a leaf warbler
strums a stranger's body like a harp.
His fingers travel over her skin as he apologizes
to heaven on a cross around his neck.

We can't unwrite our histories, we will hurt, and we will heal—
our nests, bowls of moonlight, the years will undo.

Like Any Woman

The sheets have begun to smell of sex,
      the musky breath of perfume and permission.

In every room we stay I imagine its previous tenants,
a woman slipping off her red leather pumps,

a man dropping his watch and coins on the nightstand.
      Like any lovers they fill and empty each other,

they sleep on separate sides of the mattress
      holding the wounds of memory close as a quilt.

At daybreak the man rises first. He kisses the woman's
      shoulder and leaves the room. He returns with apricots

and a baguette he steals a bite from on his way upstairs.
      She stands in the bathroom and studies her reflection

in the narrow mirror. Like any woman, she cannot decide
      if she is monstrous or beautiful.

Journal Entry, Paris

In the Jardin du Luxembourg under a canopy of elms,
a men's choir sings Simon and Garfunkel's lines
Hello darkness my old friend...

the music takes me back twenty years
to the first time I visited Paris—
how our lives get divided and categorized,
France with two different husbands.

Have I changed, what am I still looking for?
I write about Rodin's statue of Stendhal,
whether to light candles in Sainte-Chapelle,
and the quest for gifts for my daughters,

who weren't yet conceived on my first visit.
Now they want t-shirts with the names of pubs,
earrings from the shop on the bridge over the Seine.

I return to the market square where twenty years ago
I squeezed a peach to check for ripeness—
the shop owner slapped my hand,
finding the best peach for the customer was his job.
I apologized in my limited French and bought nothing.

Paul and I made mistakes all over the city—
I got trapped entering the Métro,
a waitress reprimanded him for spearing a pickle
from the jar on the café table with his fork.

I talk about *Val and Paul* as just another couple,
hiding parts of themselves, hoping
they would be the ones to return to Paris in twenty years.

I want a moving ending for this story,
words that lift off with an indelible image,
but all I have is the truth—Paul died, we buried him,
the church was filled with yellow lilies.

Dark Red Leaves

my wings are closed and I cannot fly
—Nadia Anjuman, *Dark Red Flower*

Outside, a few red leaves dangle,
guests at the sad, bright end of a party.
Autumn's loss sneaks up on me.

I watch for a small brown bird,
but the sparrow is gone—
its wings beat only inside these lines.

It's November. I'm fifty-six years old.
My daughters are both taller than I.
They are the reason I still pray.

My husband kisses my neck
before he leaves the house.
His tenderness devastates me.

Clothes in the dryer tumble to a stop,
I think how I'm like the laundry—
warm, damp, settled and wrinkled.

I want to squeeze this morning
like a grapefruit, savor its fierce juice.
My independence is not a sin.

This is the only day in the year
the sun will break at just this angle,
and nothing will ruin this hour—

not leaf blowers, not unfolded laundry.
My hand, so full of words,
can write anything, anything.

Small Blue Room

It takes a long time to get the ruins right.
                    —Jack Gilbert, *Ruins and Wabi*

Your first language was static,
          a classical radio station that never tuned in,
my first language was winter,
                    a constant searching for fire.

          My hair once draped like soft curtains
                              across your collarbone,
now I sleep in a small blue room,
                    the breeze through an open window,
          my only guest.

          Can you tell I've been reading Gilbert again:
                    a thousand colors from white to silver,
          and *Only Pittsburgh is more than Pittsburgh—*

he understood the subtle mythology,
                    the fiction and nonfiction of any marriage,
          how finally it becomes an unwinnable war.

          I tell my therapist,
our marriage was a wildflower of impulsive choices,
          our own bible of astounding mistakes—

it would take too many expensive minutes
          to explain how I chose this blue room
                    but still listen for your sleeping breath
          and imagine your chest,

lifting then falling
          like the laboring bow of a cello.

Something Holy in the World

A new student draws her hand across her shoulder
to remind me her name is Kazmir, like a sweater.
Her gesture stays with me all afternoon,
      intimate as wool on skin—silent as a Trappist monk.

The faint quickening of my child in my womb
was the moment I knew I'd leave something holy in the world—
a daughter shook the bars of my ribcage, swimming in that lake.
      We all begin in silence.

Now my hands are the spotted bark of a silver birch,
the way everyone's bodies move toward kindling.
I'm tired of being sad over what I've lost—
      it's as wrong as saying I'm tired of living.

The only woman I ever knew who killed herself
did it when I was pregnant. She gave me baby shoes for Christmas.
She graduated in June, drove to a motel and slit her throat.
      My daughter wore those shoes the day she first walked.

October has always said, *it's just you and death,*
though tonight it's still warm enough to sit on the porch—
the maple tree glows like a circus tent,
      a rodeo of red and yellow leaves.

At Edward Hopper's Self-Portrait

My father wore that same fedora, brown felt, wide brim,
fifty-five years ago when he would navigate his Plymouth

through the tangled braid of L.A. traffic, peddling life insurance
to people now dead. Every December he'd send his clients

Christmas cards with Audubon calendars inside, color plates
of indigo buntings pecking at worms, white-crowned pigeons

nesting in strangler figs. At eighty-four my father is stooped,
a slow, gray emperor penguin. This visit, which we cannot

know will be his last, he is hoping to sight a northern cardinal.
We stand together scanning the winter landscape. Like a Hopper

painting, bare maples against a watercolor sky, our backs
to the viewer—two small figures in the stillness. Not one bird.

Manzanita

I was always part manzanita, seductive limbs,

bittersweet berries, my daughters' slippery bodies

birthed into the knowing hands of midwives.

We were educated by wildfire, drunk on the gin

and tonic scent of ceanothus. How can we not

come from where we came? Chaparral, dry heat,

Western diamondbacks coiled like skinny gods

around our ankles—our hair, lousy with sparrows.

AFTERNOON

We needed to say something. We did our best. There wasn't enough time.
—Carole Maso, *The Art Lover*

We Speak of August

Alone in my kitchen, I copy
a chicken salad recipe from a Woman's Day magazine
and plan tomorrow night's dinner.

We don't know what will happen
between one raindrop and the next,
yet we speak of August as if it were a contract,
a promise the sky made.

When I was twenty-five I married a drummer
and silenced him with disapproval.

After the drummer, I married a poet—
he read aloud on the porch
and petted my head like a puppy.

My daughters grew tall as honeysuckle and left—
they took their soft skin, their buttermilk biscuit smell,
the endless hungers that organized my days.

My domain has shrunk to the narrow bone of my ankle.

I did what was asked.
I did what I feared.
Like every woman I have ever known,
I became my mother.

I stroll through the rows of houses and yards;
above me a skein of geese break in and out of formation,
fluid as laundry on a line.

Other women are out walking their dogs,
murmuring to the mothers inside their heads.

In the eastern sky the first star is out,
preparing for the long night of wishes.

At dusk every flower looks blue.

It's a Sad Story

You know the one where the couple lives together
for twenty years until he leaves her
for his dead brother's widow—
they divorce, he marries the widow,
then nine months later, he dies too.
Like *Hamlet*, minus the poison in King Hamlet's ear.

It's hard to talk about without sounding bitter—
even our daughters joke,
That's when my father married my aunt,
and I became my own cousin.
It's the story I take out on the third date
if a man asks to know more.
I can't just say *my husband died,*
or forever after I'd be lying.

The beginning was sweet,
the way beginnings can be—
we got together right after I finished high school.
All summer I listened to him sing and play guitar
at this Mexican restaurant where the waitress
was kind enough to serve me Kahlúa and creams
I'd sip like a hummingbird—barely
eighteen years old, drunk on infatuation,
Simon and Garfunkel covers, and coffee liqueur.

When I moved away to college,
he sent me letters on thin blue stationery—
he pasted one-cent stamps all over the envelopes,
drew pictures, and quoted from poems.
I've carried that box of letters with me
every place I've ever lived.

And our marriage, like any other—
groceries and children, spaghetti and laundry,
except we had music,
he'd play piano and we'd sing
I am an old woman named after my mother,
my old man is another child that's grown old.

Now I'm the old woman in the song writing this letter to you—
studying my life like I'm at a market choosing plums,
weighing my ripeness against my bruises,
offering whatever sugar might be left.

My Waitressing Days

I can see it, the apartment one flight above Santa Barbara Street

where we first lived together eating our meals in the tiny

dining room, staring at palm trees and the green hills dotted

with red tile rooftops. I can still picture the poster of blue irises

in the white kitchen, the tile fireplace, and the double bed

where our bodies curled like a treble clef, my feet warm

against your calves. Can a city haunt someone? Or maybe just

that studio, those nineteenth century walls that once held a brothel,

a school for unwed mothers, and countless tenants who also

watched every weather through those wavy glass panes.

When we moved in, I bought a ceramic candle holder I kept

on the hearth, one of so few purchases I made back in my

waitressing days. Every time I lit a candle, I felt wealthy. Years

later I looked for it, but it had disappeared the way things do.

The Language of Waitresses, 1979

I wear a red polyester dress that laces in front
(think bodice or wench)
with a pair of ruffled underpants
(think baby doll or can-can dancer).
I'm almost twenty-two and aware of my effect on men.

The bar is down a long hall—
I balance pink ladies and tequila sunrises
on a round cork tray, dodging drunk guests
and other waitresses.
I flirt shamelessly, an autopilot of smiles
and one-line comebacks.
I pretend to listen to every story and dumb joke
as I run through the list of specials in my head.
The manager propositions me,
he says *sleeping with one woman*
your whole life is like eating only vanilla ice cream.
I kindly decline then serve dinner to his wife and kids.

Tonight the fried chicken is underdone,
the line cook tells me to give the meat
a little *radar love.*
He tells me to *86* the halibut
and asks me to refill his Coke.
On my break, I eat the same salad from the salad bar
and stop a run in my nylons with clear nail polish
I borrow from Sharon
(a woman who has waited tables for thirty years).
Sharon says *you could do something more with your hair,*
Sweetheart, and hints at the wisdom of push-up bras.

At the end of my shift,
I spend thirty minutes on *side work*—
marrying ketchup bottles,

filling salt and peppers, slicing lemons.
The busboy hoses down the rubber floor mats
under the fluorescent light,
the cook blasts Foreigner's
Feels Like the First Time from the kitchen radio.
I clock out at 11:15 and drive home in my Plymouth Arrow.
I sit alone at the kitchen table,
(my hair smells like greasy fish, my feet ache).
I count my tips—
I smooth the short stacks of dirty wrinkled ones,
I build my little coin towers.

Into Dusk

Under the weight of gray clouds, slow fiddle notes

escape from a nearby pub. Heavy Irish sky.

Here is the line that tries to stop the woman

from marrying the man who wants her

to cook dinner every night. For the rest of time.

Here is the woman who says *I cannot stay with you,*

the man who answers *Stay with me anyway.*

Follow the winding path through St Stephen's Green.

Into dusk. Trapped toy boats circle the silver lake

beneath sprawling hawthorns. Weeping ash.

Here is the poem their bodies write on each other.

Anyway. Line over line in the Dublin night.

A Colder Country

We never made it to Canada, never drove the five hours
and crossed into a colder country.

We formed our own cold country.

Airplanes lift off this moment rising into blind clouds,
airplanes that could falter and descend—
whole lifetimes erased in black salt water.
We are those airplanes, those blind clouds.

A door is an imaginary obstacle.
It stops us like the painted-shut window in my kitchen,
the one I scrape with a letter opener, pressing metal into wood—
like the work of leaving a marriage, leaving a house,
shedding them—a cicada molting,
until its empty shell tumbles light across the lawn.

The door was open all along.
I passed through—took your eleven years,
your ice floes, your North Carolina,
every Colorado and long Nebraska
you crossed to keep me.

My hands are diamond-less now,
I write this apology with inexpensive fingers—

I tell you the world ended,
I tell you the world did not end.

We Are Adults

I remember the young man at a bar
in Santa Monica who ordered a bloody mary
at 11 in the morning. He reminded
those on either side of him
We are adults! There are no rules!

I think of that man sometimes
when I need permission
to enter a restaurant on my own,
to scoot up to the bar and ask for a drink.

I forget how old I am every single day.

A few years ago, a little girl stopped me
on the sidewalk and asked
if I was a grandmother. I wasn't yet,
and when I asked why she thought so,
she said, *your hair.*

My hair, the silver of burned-out campfires,
the silver of decades-old dimes,
smooth between my fingers,
the year impossible to make out.

Of course. Many people think I have been old for years.

I am a grandmother now,
and I can't go back in time.
The cliché is to say *I wouldn't want to.*

But I do want another *first* first kiss.

And at times, I even want a newborn
to latch onto my breast, to release
the cramp in my womb that says *you will suffer,*
that says *your body is this infant's home,*
that says *you will mean what love means*
to someone else forever.

Outside the Pawn Shop

I

Outside the pawn shop of lost people and stolen watches,
I see a line of poetry in pink chalk curling across the sidewalk—
I would die for you, Fiona, I would die.

On another Wednesday of kisses remembered,
I learn about three unrelated miracles—
to be born, we overcome five hundred million sperm,

the clouds above our heads weigh as much
as one hundred elephants, and in every culture across the world,
children find a way to play hide and seek.

II

At eighteen, I promise never to write love in a poem,
at twenty-six, I tell you I'll stay with you always,
at forty-four, I pawn my wedding ring for ninety-five dollars.

I believed in your consonance and your dissonance,
how you'd sing me into your body. I believed the sweat of sex
made us holy. *Are you listening? Are you there?*

You filled me with a grapefruit light—
I relished the times you called me *sweetheart,*
I didn't notice how frost sneaks in, I didn't believe in winter.

III

Somewhere a gaggle of children runs away
from each other and disappears while one calls out
Ready or not, here I come!

Before we understood sorrow, we'd practice losing people
and searching for them—alone under elephant clouds,
      we'd look behind every rock, behind even the skinniest tree.

New Year's Day in the Studio

January first is cold where I am.
I stay home to grade essays
and discover a plagiarist in the bunch.

A student from China whose sentences
usually sound distinct and foreign
as lost travelers, suddenly produces
paragraphs lucid as the *New York Times*.

I write to my student—
A lack of academic integrity
can get you expelled from college.

But what about politicians and Wall Street,
countless cheaters rewarded for their schemes,
making more money than I ever will—
I laugh at the irony.

My mother calls and reminds me to eat cabbage
for prosperity in the coming year.
She must not believe my little wealth
has always been in the stories I tell.

The gas wall heater is on full blast
in my studio apartment. It only heats
a three-foot radius, but every time I walk by,
it reminds me of the winter
my second daughter was born—

the chilly bedroom, Sophie curled
on my chest like a sea otter pup.
In the space heater's orange glow,

I slept the terrified, elated half-sleep
of every new mother, murmuring
impossible promises into her hair.

Doll, It All Goes by So Fast

for Edward Gnup (1921-2015)

I

As a child, my father was often hungry. His father
worked in a Pittsburgh steel mill for fifty cents an hour.
My father never complained about growing up poor,
but one time he mentioned how he would have loved
to take ballet lessons. He wanted to be a dancer,
instead, he played baseball in high school, enlisted
in the military, graduated college on the GI Bill,
and spent the next fifty years selling life insurance.

II

The only World War II story my father ever told
was about his last job, discharging soldiers in the Air Force.
When it was finally his turn to fly home from England,
another airman begged to take my father's place on the flight.
My father gave him the last seat on the plane—
the plane that flew into the side of a mountain.
Everyone was killed. Generosity saved my father's life,
though he didn't tell the story that way.

III

After already knowing each other for forty years,
my Polish Catholic father, who wasn't dramatic,
who seemed to have no mystical leanings at all,
shocked my mother on a walk through Vienna
saying in a previous life he'd been a Viennese Jew.
She tells me, *the first time he was in Vienna,*
he knew exactly where the synagogue was—
he found his way across Austria without a map.

IV

When I was ten, I found a copy of *The Sensuous Man*
hidden in my father's sock drawer. I was shocked at the content,
alarmed that he'd seen it too. Several years later,
he picked me up from the eighth-grade dance—
he caught me kissing my boyfriend and waited outside to give us
       privacy.
I felt that mix of shame and sorrow
we feel watching our parents witnessing us grow up.
I wasn't his baby anymore—I was a girl capable of making out.

V

My father packed my lunches all through elementary school
and junior high. He'd make cheese or liverwurst sandwiches
I'd be embarrassed to eat in front of my friends.
He'd wait up for me when I went out during high school
and fall asleep reading on the couch. I'd come home
and apologize for waking him up. He'd say *I wasn't sleeping,*
I was just resting my eyes. He never told me he loved me,
but he loved me.

VI

Before the world realized it was the most objectified,
sexist nickname, my father called me *doll.*
My whole life.
When he used this endearment, the feminist in me
chose to overlook it. I felt pretty and protected—
I knew it was politically incorrect, but I loved it.
The last cogent words he ever spoke to me were
Doll, it all goes by so fast.

VII

My father wasn't a writer. His stories ended
years ago when dementia stole his language, his body,
his life. He died at home in the living room
on my mother's eighty-eighth birthday—
my parents had been married for sixty-five years.
Work, daughters, grandkids, hiking, the ballet,
friends over for dinner—it was an unremarkable life.
And it was astonishing.

I Fake My Way Through the Days

And then the angels forget to pray for us
  —Leonard Cohen, *So Long, Marianne*

Cohen knew how abandoned I would feel in December,
when wind rides through me on a carriage.
I fake my way through the days and the lessons,
I still dream bad waitress dreams,
burnt toast and taking the martini to the wrong table.
Someone is always angry; someone wants to cut my hair.
I write the wrong seasons, I write the curled lip
of the redhead who hired me at the Eggception.
The menu must have had eighty omelets,
but all I remember is the day I dropped
a gallon bottle of burgundy on my foot.
I could tell you everything I don't know about Shakespeare,
it would take me much longer than these twelve minutes.
I remember making up how many stairs
were in the Pittock Mansion when I gave people tours of the museum.
They listened and tilted their heads like they were studying for a test.
I think of angels and December, not yet winter,
Leonard Cohen taking months and months to write his poems.
The sky is the white of the day Paul died,
the way the sky remembers sorrow.
I don't want to invite his ghost back,
but I'll tell you his death is the scar between my before and after,
everything after happens in a place a little bit above ground,
where I invent the number of stairs,
what Shakespeare taught us of tragedy,
and how the angels knew where the martini went.

EVENING

The wrens build at dusk. Friends, I love their moss-dressed nests twisting in the pitch of the rafters, for they have taught me that the ruins of the dance are the dance.

—Joseph Fasano, *Hymn*

A Thousand Possible Clouds

Go find a pencil
the world is a terrible first draft.

When you write a story, you have choices—
horizon, chickweed, loneliness,

a copse of trees harbors soldiers
stealthily as a virus invades a body

or holds redwoods, gentle as grandparents,
collecting their centuries in a map of pale rings.

Listen, a foghorn beyond the fields
moans like an animal suffering

the sky has surrendered its hours
or exploded into a thousand possible clouds.

The children on the road far behind you
have lost their parents, their country—

someone got too greedy,
someone believed he knew what was right.

Or they're your children on that road
carrying home blackberries to make cobbler—

cut the butter into the flour, stop to kiss
the swirled crowns of their heads.

The Work of Flying

Name a poet who doesn't write of death, and I'll tell you
that poet isn't writing poems. Death waits in each of us—

our hungry imaginations, the cello notes of midnight clocks,
high red-cheeked fevers that drag our mothers to their knees.

Stand at the ocean, feel your insignificance, the way everyone
facing the water first discovers how small they truly are.

Listen to the tango mewing of the hundred circling gulls—
remember when you learned how they mate for life, a goal

you could not accomplish. Watch them turn the work of flying
into an improbable dance—dropping then catching themselves,

over and over, the way for a moment between each footstep
your whole body is balanced on something slender as a wing.

November, Berlin

Near the entrance to the U-Bahn, a young man leans
on the dirty tiles singing Leonard Cohen's *Hallelujah*,
his battered guitar case reminds you of the canvas suitcase

your grandfather packed when he emigrated from Poland—
one change of clothing and a bundle of letters from a girl,
pages of onion skin he'd read every night to the dark waves.

At your feet, a Stolperstein, a stumbling stone—
Here lived Charlotte Wolff, murdered in Riga.
Hier wohnte Charlotte Wolff, ermordet in Riga, 1942,

her only obituary, a brass plate tucked among cobblestones,
etched with her name, her dates, and where her life ended.
A skinny pigeon searches the ground for anything living.

You, too, wander the streets, crossing the invisible
scar that dissects this city—is it always November
in Berlin where history and longing sing the same song?

Another stone, *Hier wohnte Max Sittner, ermordet, 1943*—
perhaps during his morning prayers, German soldiers pushed
into Max's frigid apartment, lied about a spa in Theresienstadt.

And another—Asta Raesener, twenty years old in 1941.
Was Asta cooking soup for her mother and father, stirring
the broth, slicing their only potato thinner and thinner?

Her Face, Crimson Petals

for Du'a Khalil Aswad, a 17-year-old Iraqi Kurd girl stoned to death in an honor killing for her relationship with a Sunni Muslim boy.

Afterwards
an uncle gathers her in his arms
    like kindling
the body takes so long to surrender—
a palm tree straining its skinny roots
for the chance to stand.

Once she watched her boyfriend
nurse a wounded parakeet—
    he fed the small green bird
grapes and sunflower seeds
until it flew from the sill.

    What is honor?

A father teaches his son
to skip stones on a lake,
    across the gray water
they watch the smooth pebbles
splash and leap.

    There are no bad stones,
only the world reborn in us
    each morning,
the question of rain or no rain.

Lament of a Bare Branch

dedicated to the bare branches: young men
who will never marry or become fathers

On my way home, I will not steal a red pear for my wife.
I will not place a ring of kisses on the throat of my wife.

She will not pour my ginger tea or stir steaming noodles.
I will not watch her watch clouds dress the moon, my wife.

In our bath, she will not wash my head, chest or ankles.
I will not softly trace the gentle hills of her spine, my wife.

I will not gather our babies like fat bushels of sweet grain.
She will not lift their hungry mouths to her breast, my wife.

At the stream, I will not draw herons beside our children.
She will not find crickets hidden in their hands, my wife.

Like a branch in wet snowfall, I will not bow in sorrow.
When she leaves this world, I will not bow for my wife.

I will curl around myself in sleep, as wolves do in winter.
I will not tell the dragon stories of my dreams to my wife.

The Cries of One Crow

The cries of one crow can destroy a morning—
    somewhere in the world there is always a war.

At Arlington National Cemetery the headstones
    rise like white birch stumps in a ruined forest,

armed guards protect the Unknown Soldier,
    though what human does not go unknown?

In the National Liberation Museum in Groesbeek,
    a Dutch sculptor carves clay soldiers climbing

from their graves, smiling figures offer each other
    a hand. Cutting down a tree will not kill its roots.

One crow can torment an entire neighborhood—
    whose childhood is not scrabbled in violence,

each plastic grenade an education in war?
    The tally of the dead rises like snowmelt in a river,

I cannot unwrite their stories, unbury their graves.
    I can only reach for the warmth of my own daughters,

and imagine the parents who wait for a soldier
who will never come home. Somewhere in the world

a forest recovers, a stump is sprouting new growth—
    give one child a branch, he creates a weapon

give another child a branch, he raises his hands
    to conduct a symphony only he will hear.

Memory of Forests

I cannot speak of disappearing trees
the way I cannot say the names of people I have lost
look up, adore her crown, her canopy
holding back sky for another's sunlight
imagine her intimate map of roots
underground communion
what of murder trees, widow makers crushing loggers
wind-toppled eucalyptus flattening homes

do not punish what is wild for its wildness

wind-toppled eucalyptus flattening homes
widow makers crushing loggers
underground communion
her intimate map of roots
hold back sky, adore her crown
say the names of trees we've lost, tall thin prayers

giant sequoia, Gowen cypress, *maple-leaf oak*

Shadows in Gold

Como una sombra de oro
En el trigal te disuelves.

Like a shadow in gold
You dissolve in the wheat.
—Federico García Lorca, *Four Ballads in Yellow*

In Calexico the separated linger at the fence.
Brother and sister press hungry fingers to cheeks
between the sharp wires, this sparrow's kiss
—a brief shower in the desert's mean heat.

An uncle, *un tío,* pushes a gift through the gap;
a husband delivers a week's pay to a grateful
wife. And many never risk the difficult trip,
afraid of the lawless rifles of the border patrol.

A Mexican woman whispers to her grown son,
Es la linea de reuniones de amor—the border
of loving reunions, the narrow altar between
one country of disappearing families and another.

Who doesn't wait for such a reunion? Parted not
by borders, but the proud rivers of our own hearts.

On the Corner of Powell and César Chávez

The welfare office squats in a strip mall
beside a manicure salon,
a convenience market that doubles as a bar,

and an auto parts store that allows customers
to work on their cars in the parking lot.

All day amid scattered cigarette butts,
guys sprawl on their backs under their engines,
cussing.

The building has a red awning,
like an old-time ice cream parlor or a river boat.
Trash collects near the door—
Jack in the Box bags and paper Starbucks cups.

Nearby, U-Haul, Public Storage and Instant Loans,
everything people need to leave here
or to find a way to stay.

It's the saddest street in town,
the kind of place you could live two blocks from
and never notice.

*

The woman in front of me is barefoot.
It is December,
her hands are red, cracked, filthy.

She recites the long, sad lyric
of her shattered family,
begs me to help
get her child back.

She is at the wrong office.

She is high,
perhaps psychotic—

she may not even have a child.

*

In this room full of children
who didn't ask for these parents—
a bleached blonde, deep cleavage,
hugely pregnant, tells me offhandedly,

I have so much to do.
I just got out of rehab.

A distracted mother
feeds her toddler *Flamin' Hot Cheetos*
for breakfast,
a father, with devil horns
tattooed on his forehead,
says he's looking for work—

all I can do is nod, but the fierce crow
in me wants to say to them—

Your children will become you.
Who would hire you?
I wouldn't get a tattoo from you.

*

After my break I schedule an appointment
for a 22-year-old mother of four,
seven thousand miles from her native Pakistan.

She can't read English.
She has come to this office
asking for anything we can do.
It's the simplest, most human request—
anything.

Her hands rest on the desk, a sculpture,
intricate black mehndi petals and vines
swirl across her palms.

In this run-down office
of Miley Cyrus T-shirts, dirty pajama bottoms
and homemade swastika tattoos,
in her flowing silk hijab, she is incandescent, iconic—
I want to call her a lotus blossom
rising from such deep mud,
but she's nobody's flower—
more like a redwood or a wolf.

We will issue her money to buy food,
not enough for a family of six,
but it is something.

                    *

Another woman
pleads with me to replace her food stamp card,
tells me I look like Helen Hunt—
a creative attempt to charm me.

State policy is to mail the card to the client's home
if it's lost or stolen,

but she has no address.

Her only photo identification
is an inmate ID.
She looks worse in person,
scabby and sharp as death.

I can see this is her 44th EBT card,
they are her only currency—
bartered for crack or meth.
When I hand her a new card,
her breath, yeasty,
her few teeth, gray,
she announces,
God bless you in the name of Jesus Christ.
Loud, so everyone turns to watch,
she says it again
and tucks the card in her bra.
She cannot leave fast enough.

Another Morning at the Welfare Office

8:00 am

Today the lobby feels like a cocktail party.

Clients rarely bring books to the welfare office.

Aladdin is playing on the TV,
strains of *A Whole New World* fill the room.

I'm at the reception desk by eight,
people already lined up between the ropes
like they're waiting for a Ferris wheel.

My first client is an exotic dancer,
in the shortest shorts possible,
bleeding from her neck.

Her legal name is Baby.
She is a mother of three children
with three absent fathers.

My next client, a young woman in sunglasses and a wig,
using an alias,
is hiding from a man who beat and raped her
in front of their four-year-old son.

*

I can hear two strangers commiserate over the waiting list
for Section 8 Housing;

two more argue which homeless shelter
serves the best food;

and it seems someone is always mentioning
a person they know who cheats the system.

But every single hour

while the rest of the city
sip chai lattes at coffee houses
or eat over-priced panini at trendy cafes,

someone sits across from me
          who is hungry.

The newspaper calls it food insecurity—

          it looks like terror.

                    *

Between clients
I sneak jelly beans into my mouth
to reassure myself
I have enough;
there will be enough.

                    9:00 am

A woman in a black burqa,
only her eyes visible
behind their narrow window,

leans across my desk
and asks
Where can I get free birth control?

I can see on her case,
she has six children under ten.

I slip her Planned Parenthood's number.

Her husband is ten feet away.
She glances in his direction
and whispers

If he hears us, he will beat me.
Contraception is frowned upon;
wife abuse, it seems, is not.
She's thirty-two years old
and moves like a grandmother.

10:00 am

A girl, my daughter's age,
comes to the desk.

She twists her long, dark hair,
and stares at me.

She tells me her friend filled out her paperwork
for her.

The application asks:

     Last grade completed?
the friend has written a null sign.

When I inquire, she admits

I didn't get to go.
She tells me she is from a family of gypsies,
who do not believe in educating their girls.

In this country, in this century,
she never attended school.

I ask for her signature.
She clutches her social security card
and carefully copies

each letter of her name.

11:00 am

The State closes people's food stamp cases
when they are incarcerated—

clients are forced to return to this office
and confess
they've been locked up.

The woman at my desk seems friendly, a stubbed-out cigarette
tucked behind her ear,

rhinestones glued to her acrylic fingernails.

I break the unspoken rule
and ask why she went to jail.

She answers, *Oh, just a PV—*

as if people in the regular world
should know a Probation Violation
when they hear one.

She shrugs and says,
Once they got ya, they got ya.

*

I want to press harder,
ask what put her in jail the first time,

but there are questions
you never ask:

Why do you stay with him,
when he throws you
downstairs?

Do you need another baby,
when you can't support
the five (or seven or ten)
you already have?

And why all those tattoos
on your face?

*

I won't talk about
the acrid smell
of body odor,
urine and mildew
that lingers in the lobby,
clinging to the homeless and their sad bags
of everything.

I won't admit
some days I'm toxic with judgment,
calling clients
nut jobs and rodeo clowns
behind their backs.

I check my personal email
and count the minutes till lunch.

12:00 pm

On my lunch break I take a walk.

Across the street
a Somali woman leaves Safeway
with two bags full of groceries
balanced on top of her head.

Graceful as an egret,
she crosses
the highland plateau in her memory,
she speaks into a phone
tucked between her hijab and cheek.

At noon on the corner of Pepe's Sandwiches
and Quick Cash Checks,
the world is full of every poverty
and every wealth.

I wait for the light.

Before We Speak

Before we speak of today's plague,
we must kneel and say thirty-five million prayers
for everyone lost in the forgotten plague—
the AIDS plague so many of us cruelly connected
with sin and shame, the plague another man
in power took too long to pronounce,

carried on the shoulders of love
or in the hidden cells of the bloodstream,
black and ruinous as the one spread by fleas
on the backs of rats scuttling across previous centuries.

Before we speak of today's plague,
we must lift up the memory of those who died
in pest houses, fever sheds, isolated and terrified,
dying from epidemics that feast on poverty—

cholera, tuberculosis, typhoid,
all the viral and bacterial plundering
that destroyed whole continents and changed
the direction the planet would spin.

When we finally do speak of today's plague,
we must sculpt a plague column
tall enough to reach the toes of heaven,
permanent as granite or marble—

built of sorrow and a thousand late apologies
for all the misplaced blame and the hundred ways
this plague could have been prevented.

But death's violin was always playing
outside our window—even now,
Apollo's random arrows fly, aimed at you or at me

as we hope for an improbable mercy,
unlikely as snowdrops blooming in February,
thin green stems bursting through frozen ground.

Fall Like Petals

Every morning across the thirsty world,
women and children spend their lives

walking miles to carry clean water home—
the trail we follow becomes our story.

Lost voices, lost learning,
no science, no art, and no chance

to rise from poverty's empty well.
Imagine a bouquet of giant blossoms,

five-gallon buckets balanced on their heads,
bending the slender stems of their necks.

Here at the end of time,
my words only skim the surface, a Jesus lizard.

I want the rain to fall like petals
every morning across the thirsty world.

Song for Ukraine

Kyiv trembles like an old man
clutching his cane but insisting he walk.
A child presses against a chain link fence
searching for his lost mother.
Five men carry a marble sculpture of Jesus
to hide in a bunker, stone palms outstretched,
a hole in the center of each one.
A man plays piano for refugees,
each note clear as glass.

Each note clear as glass,
a man plays piano for refugees,
a hole in the center of each one.
To hide in a bunker, stone palms outstretched,
five men carry a marble sculpture of Jesus
searching for his lost mother.
A child presses against a chain link fence
clutching his cane but insisting he walk.
Kyiv trembles like an old man.

Cherries

Looking at the fist-sized bunch
        of U-pick cherries I just pitted,
        each with its rough gaping hole,

red juice spilling on the plate, for a moment
        I see bodies stacked on a battlefield,
        shot through and bloody.

It's too early in the morning
        for these kinds of graphics—
        I blame all the years I taught two profoundly

anti-war novels to sixteen and seventeen-year-olds—
        The Things They Carried
        and *All Quiet on the Western Front,*

my brief and truest lecture:
        War is an immeasurable waste.
        I know I offended some students

whose relatives died in uniform.
        I promise you, I take nothing away
        from anyone's service or sacrifice,

I only judge the deeply flawed answer
        the world relies on when words are bootless,
        and cherries come cheap.

Czech Angels

for Eleanor Gnup (1927-2022)

> *I'd like to die listening to a piece of music.*
> —Robert Walser, *Masquerade and Other Stories*

I always imagine it will be December when I die,
perhaps I'll be doing something I've done many times

like buttering toast for breakfast, or maybe I'll die like
Walser, walking in Christmas snow. Three years ago

when I visited Prague, I was drawn to the Czech angels,
they were everywhere—flying in Renaissance paintings,

carved from granite in overgrown cemeteries, wearing
bronze wings in St. Vitus Cathedral. I took photos

of each one, as if they were my cousins or old friends.
I like to think when I die, those angels will remember—

they'll gather my body and carry me to the angel hotel,
where the bread is sweet and the music, even sweeter.

MIDNIGHT

Strange dogs came to the yard
And howled under my window all night.
It was a bad time for the heart.
  —Anna Akhmatova, *By the Seashore*

When We Were Horses

      We knew only the mad gallop across uneven earth,
      the muddy real estate that calls to every animal.

No one could tell us how each step relied on the integrity of tendons,
the scissored geometry of stifle and fetlock.

      We inhabited our wildness.
      We stood on all four legs, unaware that the map
      of our blood depended on it.

We did not understand our own fragile design,

      how our delicate ankles might shatter
      under the heft of our glorious anatomy,

how life can become
a cracked cannon bone or fractured pastern.

      We grazed timothy and bluegrass
      we dreamed our apple and carrot dreams.

Resurrected

The mud puddle that splashes your white linen trousers

or the thorn that snags your wool sweater as you pass,

these are not problems; these are what your grandmothers

would call *the stuff of life*. Your morning walk, the steep climb,

perspiring and pausing to catch your breath: a gift. Even fighting off

gophers that roil and rumple your pristine lawn: the earth is theirs.

Enjoy their progress. And don't speak of needing resurrection,

you are resurrected. Roll back that stone. Go be holy.

Winter of Rain

When all the stars have finally fallen,
their small flames blown out like a child's first wish,
the world stumbling in darkness,
then I can write you the unwritable poem,
    the impossible prayer I never could pray.

Like a river moving through an ocean
or a giant sequoia holding century-old stories,
I told you and did not tell you
your mind was quick as any comet,
    your eyes, the color of earth after a winter of rain.

I would have been satisfied with so little—
to feel your thigh pressed against my thigh,
the way strangers sit close on a crowded train,
to know one moment of your terrible power,
    your animal warmth.

My silence is louder than a Sunday morning choir,
a hundred voices praising a beloved, imaginary god,
passionate hymns filling an abandoned heaven—
my silence holds you closer
    than anyone else's arms.

More Than Sparrows

Fear not, the Bible says you are worth more
than many sparrows,

though your face is a study in accordioned lines,
scissored switchbacks, and eucalyptus bark—

a galaxy of abandoned planets.

Trees communicate underground—
in their silent poetry of fungal filaments,
sequoias and aspens can save each other.

It seems those who stop loving us
ruin our landscapes, clear-cut our forests,
unaware of the destruction they leave.

When you were younger, time moved slowly,
trouble arrived on the evening news—

now, you can barely keep up with the sorrow.

Every morning you still write a name
in the condensation on your bathroom mirror—

you can see yourself so clearly in the letters
before they disappear into the sink.

Pink Peonies

I watch a news clip of Chinese couples
recreating their weddings.
Married during the Cultural Revolution,
the government forbid them to dress up or be photographed.

An elderly woman, in red lipstick, wearing a white gown
carries a bouquet of pink peonies and smiles like a new bride
beside her husband of fifty years.

*

Who will stand beside me?
I'm tired of not being known,
tired of telling people *I'm fine, I'm better, I'm happy.*

I am all those things, and I'm half a heart,
cold feet in bed, an empty chair at the table.

*

I never imagined this life,
teaching high school again,
living in this studio where people come visit
and walk straight into my bedroom
which is also my living room, office, and den.

Most days I hold my words back from the world.
I can't tell my students how I really feel—good or bad.
When I laugh wildly, they tilt their heads like confused dogs,
surprised I'm actually human.

*

We don't see each other, and then in a moment we do—
a stranger on the train last night looked at me and mouthed,
You okay? I almost wept for such unexpected kindness.

*

I leave my house and am tempted to wave goodbye
to my laptop, the way I would a husband or a child.
My computer sits on my thighs so much of any day
it feels alive as a baby or a puppy,
my constant companion in the imaginary world.

*

I tell my students that before GPS
most of my fights were in cars with men
too proud to stop and ask for directions.

I miss the crinkle and possibility of a paper map,
the days when arriving at a new destination
felt like an achievement, a kind of miracle—
or you got lost and ended up
somewhere even better.

Song from the Third Floor

Down on 37th Street, a truck collects
empty cans and bottles. I listen to the clatter
and watch from this chair, from this decade,

the decade I finally grew older—
my joints creaking like the crooked
wooden drawers in this kitchen.

My younger daughter calls.
Sometimes I wish I'd been born
her friend instead of her mother,

it would have been so much easier on us both.
I have no advice for her or anyone,
though I've made every possible mistake.

The doves in my chest clutch their wings
to their ribs, my featherless arms hold nothing—
I threw away a whole life to get to this window.

Next door on the back porch an old woman
hangs her blouses on a clothesline.
In the morning sun, her silver hair looks pink.

When You Are Invisible, You Can Say Anything

At two in the morning through plaster walls,
I hear the neighbors' whispers and groans.
I hear the thunder of helicopters—
giant blackbirds without hearts,
the wild soundtrack of urban living.

Branches outside my window are like the fingers of old women,
stiff knuckles tap on the glass.
I study my own hands, imagine secrets buried in my limbs—
tight buds waiting for April, the distant memory of leaves.

At sixty-one, I count and recount my remaining summers.
When I face anyone on the street, I notice
how their eyes slip over me without pausing.
When did I become ashamed to exist?

They tell me at this age I can say anything—
I tell you I'm losing control to the student in the back row
with the low voice who dares me to go further,
to push the invisible ropes we line up against.

I'm supposed to be his teacher—
I can't tell him I've always bounced
from one bad answer to the next wrong move,
that I've followed people across the whole country—
and what man is worth all those Tennessees?

I never had a brother but I wanted one,
wanted to catch glimpses of his hairy belly
when he would lift his shirt to scratch or stretch,
wanted to inhale the feral scent of his bedroom,
watch him shoot free throws on the driveway.

I can say I wish my father had treated me
like a man treats a young woman.
He was kind and respectful, never crossed
a line that any good life insurance salesman
wouldn't cross, but I wanted more.

I heard a man read a poem
about how he drove by a burning house,
watched the arc of water from the firefighter's hose
and silently celebrated that his own house wasn't on fire.

I tell myself remember the passions you've known,
the man with the bluest eyes in the world
lifted you onto his lap in one move,
you surrendered, ignored every commandment,
coveted strange gods, and ran into the burning house.

The Night I First Heard Cicadas

When it came to men, I had a *broken chooser.*
I couldn't tell whether their red flags meant trouble
or were embroidered linen handkerchiefs only for me.
I was grateful for every scrap I got.
I cheated with men who were married.
They wanted me, but once removed, like a cousin,
like watching a tornado on television.
I told myself their wives must be grateful for the break
from their husbands' relentless needs—
that swarm of hungry bees rattling inside so many men's pants.

My head still swirls with wrong choices,
the way the wind tears the last leaves from the sycamore,
the way saying *sycamore* turns my mouth into half a kiss
and I remember the way we kissed when we were twenty,
when it felt like we had discovered a new tribe,
a whole new species—like no one else could have invented
such spectacular tenderness.

I once chased love across the country.
The night I first heard cicadas, I thought they were electricity,
a firestorm, something dangerous as someone
who wipes a crumb from your cheek
then acts as if he's saved you from a hurricane.
I'm tired of pulling nothing out of a man
and giving it a beautiful title.

How to Survive Online Dating

after Lorrie Moore, *How to Become a Writer*

After *Serious painter1956* tells you he still hopes his art will be discovered by a big gallery, tell him you like a positive thinker, and meet him for a drink.

While you wait for your order, and he slips you just enough cash for *his* cocktail, try not to register your alarm, and don't remind him that this kind of move may have worked when he was seven (with his mom shopping for Matchbox cars at Toys RUs) but you need a man with wee bit deeper pockets.

Don't laugh out loud when *CoolJazzandSmiles* rides to the restaurant on his bicycle but doesn't own a padlock so you are forced to eat outside on the patio in December (in the rain) to keep a lookout, as bikes do get stolen all the time in Oakland, even when they are locked up.

And do not focus on his hairy little hobbit hands or his jewelry.

Feel a renewed sense of energy when *Goldenpipes4U*, who earns his living as a voice-over artist, does a brilliant imitation of the electronic voice inside an ATM. Try to stay upbeat when he gets a bit too ambitious, attempting impressions of Richard Nixon and Al Pacino, like it's 1977 and he's auditioning for the *Johnny Carson Show*.

Don't say a word as he continues to remind you that *he* paid for your drinks, as if it might be a novel occurrence, a kind of one time only *event*. Don't dwell on his cargo pants or his loud Hawaiian shirt.

You will lose hope. You will threaten to take down your profile daily.

You will tell your best friend you cannot bear to look at one more shirtless bathroom selfie, or standing in front of his car selfie, or proud big fish photo. You cannot tolerate one more balding man hiding under a wide variety of hats, no more porn star mustaches, or anything taken in the beige dust of Burning Man.

But wait! You'll get compliments:

You look good for 60!
Did you dress up just for me? You'd be gorgeous if you'd dye your hair.
So persist! Arrange a happy hour with *MtTamHiker07* who will wear
shorts to the wine bar and those Nike sneakers with individual toes,
which will make him look a little like a capybara in the wild.

But what did your mother always tell you? *Clothes don't make the man!*
Your optimism will fade when he sees the check and asks,

Why'd you choose such a pricey place?

You'll offer to pay, and he'll take you up on it.

He's saving his money for a lawyer.

You'll learn that his ex-wife has not allowed him to see their two
children since the day he revealed he wanted to *experiment* with having
other partners, he's polyamorous, which he tries to make sound noble,
or genetic—like someone born with a love of science or perfect pitch.

Your most recent date, *Realdeal57,* is charming—he makes you laugh!

(He's handsome! He speaks French!) He tells you twice he loves your
name *and* your hair. He says he'd have flirted with you at Trader Joe's, if
you'd met in real life (IRL).

But you'll get home and he'll write that he just doesn't *feel the romance.*

This is where you'll say to yourself, of course you don't believe in fairy
tales, but sitting across from *Realdeal57,* you felt like Cinderella at the
ball—except the prince apparently didn't choose you, and your golden

carriage is a Toyota Matrix from a previous decade that needs new tires and could really use a wash.

Two for Joy

Here in the belly of persimmon season,
we taste the truth. What is autumn if not
        the bright orange fruit of reckoning?

Our voices offer naked words
that have waited in our bodies for years.
        We finally got everything right.

The prayer flags have faded to pale pink.
In light wind, they flutter like a girl's silk slip,
        a quiet aria of grateful prayers.

All our lives we saw single magpies:
One for sorrow.
        At last we see two.

The weather is the temperature of mercy,
we've survived the lonely line of hours.
        We look forward to the hush of dusk.

In bed, we take each other's hand.
When one of us shifts in sleep,
        the net of our fingers holds.

We're All Tragic Heroes

If I ever move out of this house,
I'll miss the windows that let in sunset at just the right angle,
filling this studio with an apricot light—
light that makes me feel I've survived something,
and isn't survival a kind of grace?

I only know life keeps hitting us with unexpected sorrows.

No one explained how we would lose
our children at every age they pass through.

Those little humans are gone—
their sweet-smelling infant heads disappear
inside moody teenagers then anxious adults
who become photos on our walls,
rushed conversations on phones.

I too have lost myself at each age.
My skin is traitorous, my bones, brittle,
and I've replaced religion with literature—
now I believe we're all tragic heroes with fatal flaws.

I ask myself, *what is my fatal flaw?*
Am I too impulsive, too ambitious?
Or is it about still wanting to be desired?

For that, no one needs to tell me *Your stock has fallen.*
All I can do is pour a glass of wine
and wait for the light to turn to mercy.

American Meditation

Your father wakes, kisses the soft curve of your mother,
rises with faith in the man who will collect his garbage,

the woman who will deliver the mail. His America
was always a train whistle, the honor of going to work.

The sky's light behind the mountain changes from red
to blue. He walks beside a Walmart and Starbucks—

those make-believe Americas. At 84, his shoulders hunch,
he forgets to look up—the way we all forget to look up.

Your father rests beside a river as wide as hope—gold
maple leaves roil and churn in the cold foam, floating

like the faraway war dead we forget as soon as the news
is quiet. America is that river, those golden leaves too.

On his porch, any old man in a Dodgers sweatshirt,
he stares back at the last century, unable to recognize

the one he walks through now. Across the driveway
his neighbor calls out, *It's warmer today, a little warmer.*

Pieces of Days

All we have are the pieces of days we collect
like tulips in a jar on the kitchen table—

the tart taste of wine from a metal cup
on a picnic with a friend,
the way yellow chalk coated the fingers
of our favorite teacher.

We did nothing to deserve these denim skies,
the red-tailed hawk circling
like a halo above the shaken world.

Someone said every poem is an elegy,
I think every poem has a hidden stanza—

This hour under the late autumn leaves will pass,
loneliness is the room you'll return to—
but not now, not yet.

Notes

"Dark Red Leaves"
Nadia Anjuman was an Afghan poet who was murdered by her husband for
wanting to visit her sister during the final day of Ramadan. Her husband, Neia
only spent a month in prison. Nadia was survived by her six-month-old son.

"November, Berlin"
The Stolpersteine project was initiated by German artist Gunter Demnig in
1992. A Stolperstein is a ten-centimeter concrete cube bearing a brass plate
inscribed with the name and life dates of victims of Nazi extermination or
persecution. The project aims to commemorate individuals at exactly the last
place of residency–or, sometimes, work–which was freely chosen by the person
before they fell victim to Nazi terror. Literally, it means 'stumbling stone' and
metaphorically 'stumbling block'.

"Her Face, Crimson Petals"
"Honor violence is a crime that has been or may have been committed to
protect or defend the honor of the family and/or community" (Helba et
al, 2015). According to the UN Population Fund, every year about 5,000
women and girls fall victim to murders committed in the name of protecting
family honor in different parts of the world (UN State of World Population
2000, Chesler, 2010). Even more tragically, "many of them are killed for the
'dishonor' of having been raped" (UN State of World Population 2000). In
Iraq only, 150 women are killed annually, but these are only rough estimates
since many deaths are not reported. Every year 400-500 women are killed
brutally in Iran to protect men's "honor." The killers are usually close
relatives—often the victim's father, husband, or brother. According to a
report published in *The Lancet* in October 2020, at least 8,000 such killings
were reported in Iran between 2010 and 2014. "The number of honor killing
victims is greater than reported as in some cases women were driven to suicide
or the cause of the death was not reported as murder but as illness," according
to Dr. Rezvan Moghadam, founder of the Iranian organization Stop Honor
Killings.

"Lament of a Bare Branch"
The sex ratio imbalance in Asian countries persists due to male preference in
many of those cultures.

"The Cries of One Crow"
The sculpture at the National Liberation Museum in Groesbeek, the Netherlands, is by a Dutch artist, Fransje Povel-Speleers, and is called *Resurrection*.

"Shadows in Gold"
Since 2018, at least 50 migrants have died in Imperial County while attempting to cross the border, according to Border Patrol data. More migrants died from 2018 to 2020–the latest available data from the agency–than in the previous six years combined. Incomplete reporting by Border Patrol and a high number of people reported missing but never found mean the death toll could be much larger.

"Fall Like Petals"
Four billion people, almost two thirds of the world's population, experience severe water scarcity for at least one month each year. Over two billion people live in countries where water supply is inadequate. Half of the world's population could be living in areas facing water scarcity by as early as 2025. The green basilisk lizard is also called a plumed or double-crested basilisk; but its amazing ability to run on water gives this species its most recognizable moniker: the Jesus Christ lizard or Jesus lizard.

About the Author

A native of California, **Valentina Gnup** earned her MFA in Creative Writing from Antioch University Los Angeles. Her poetry has garnered many awards, including the Tucson Festival of Books Literary Award for Poetry, *Rattle*'s Reader's Choice Award, and the Lascaux Prize in Poetry. Her poems have appeared in many literary journals including *December, Brooklyn Review, Nimrod*, and *The New Guard*. She lives in Oakland, California.